Leisa Anslinger

8 WAYS TO BUILD PARISH COMMUNITY

A practical guide for ministers and parish leaders

TWENTY-THIRD PUBLICATIONS
twentythirdpublications.com

TWENTY-THIRD PUBLICATIONS
One Montauk Avenue, Suite 200
New London, CT 06320
(860) 437-3012 or (800) 321-0411
www.twentythirdpublications.com

Cover illustration: ©Shutterstock.com / AVA Bitter

ISBN: 978-1-62785-402-3
Library of Congress Control Number: 2018953650
Printed in the U.S.A.

A division of Bayard, Inc.

Contents

Introduction

How would you describe your parish? If someone were to say, "Fill in the blank. My parish is ______ ," how would you respond?

Ask the people you know to fill in the blank. Now, ask people who are at church on Sunday but whom you do not know to fill in the blank. If you're really interested, ask people who are at church to ask the people they know who are not at church to fill in the blank. What picture do the responses paint? Do people consider the parish a place that is rarely open except on Sundays, with an occasional social or service opportunity? Is your parish known as a warm and welcoming community? Are those who are involved in a ministry or group always on the lookout for others to invite to serve, or do they give the impression that no additional help is needed? Does the parish have a strong sense of mission, in which people are living and growing in faith? Is the parish like family for some, many, or most people? Did you hear all of these sorts of responses and more?

In the past fifteen years, I have often talked with parish leaders about their hopes, dreams, and prayers for their parish. The most common thing they tell me is that, no matter how much they feel their parish is growing as a community of faith, there is always more that can be done. They recognize the importance of the parish in their relationship with Christ, and they wish that others could see the tremendous impact the parish could have in their lives and faith. Many worry that their parish is aging and shrinking, and they wonder how they might better engage young people. Most also speak about how a small group of people bears responsibility for the parish through involvement and financial giving, while the majority of people come to Mass on Sunday but are otherwise disconnected from the parish. In fact, the sense that there is more to be done is in direct response to this: in many parishes, when leaders look around, they see fewer people at Mass or parish events, and the ones who do come are getting older. And even in parishes that are growing and have many young families, there still is that large number of disconnected people. Surely, they tell me, there must be a way to build a strong community in which more people are growing in faith together.

Why is this important? Because the parish is the place where people encounter Christ and grow in and express their faith through the celebration of the Eucharist and sacraments, with one another as members of Christ's body, and through ministry and outreach. In other words, the parish is where most people are evangelized and where they grow to evangelize others, leading them to a deep and fruitful relationship with Jesus Christ. Pope Francis points to this in *The Joy of the Gospel*: "The parish is the presence of the Church in a given territory, an environment for hearing God's word, for growth in the Christian life, for dialogue, proclamation, charitable outreach, worship and celebration. In all its activities the parish encourages and trains its members to be evangelizers. It is a community of communities, a sanctuary where the thirsty come to drink in the midst of their journey, and a center of constant missionary outreach" (EG, 28).

This is more than a theological statement about the role of the parish in leading people more deeply into Christ's love. This is also a practical reality, borne out by numerous studies that point to the role of the faith community in bringing people to the life of discipleship. My strong suspicion is that if you are reading this book, you know this through your own experience. Belonging within the parish leads us to grow in faith and to express our faith by sharing God's love at home, work or school, in our parish, and in the world around us.

Most of us likely experienced a similar path: coming to Mass led us to initial involvement in the parish. We may or may not have had a deep life of faith. Our involvement may have happened when we responded to an announcement at the end of Mass or in the bulletin. It is more likely that it happened when we became acquainted with someone at the parish who invited us in. It is possible that a friend invited us to participate in the parish, which led to a reigniting of faith. This early involvement connected us to other parishioners who witnessed to their faith and the satisfaction they experience in service, which led to deeper participation, resulting in increased willingness to give of ourselves and our resources. Somewhere along the way, the parish started to feel like home. And the more at home we feel in our parish—the more it becomes our family of faith—the more deeply we grow in relationship with God and commitment to

Christ, and the more we are drawn to give of ourselves and our resources to the parish and beyond it.

This leads us to an important realization. As parish leaders, we have a part to play in making our parish a true community of faith. More than this, we have a responsibility to do so. Whatever our role in the parish, as staff members or parishioner ministers, there are many ways in which we can influence how parishioners connect with one another, invite friends and family members to the parish, and lead people to become involved. Those young people your parish hopes to attract? They are more likely to come and to stay if they feel that the parish values them and wants them to belong. The many who are disconnected? The only way most will become rooted in the parish is through a warm, personal invitation carried out within a welcoming community of faith. The conviction behind the writing of this booklet is that while this may sound like an insurmountable challenge, it is actually an attainable goal.

What does it take to build community in your parish? I believe the eight ways to which this book points are a perfect beginning. This is why reading this book with other leaders will be key to reaching the goal of building the parish as a faith community.

- Start with the foundational leadership principles below.

- Read and discuss the book together, chapter by chapter. Each chapter describes one way to build community in your parish, followed by an exploration of this step of parish practice.

- Each chapter ends with practical ideas related to the step you have been exploring. These ideas are intended as a springboard for your discussions rather than an exhaustive, programmatic list.

- Make a list of current practices that align with the points in each chapter, ideas that surface for expanding on what is already working in your parish, and ways your parish might grow toward the step in the future.

- At the end of your shared reading, take time to create a plan that incorporates the ideas and strategies that emerged in your discussions.

- Explore each chapter in light of the collective experience of your group. Include others in your discussions, especially when you are thinking about an aspect of parish life in which they are involved.

- At the same time, fight the temptation to unnecessarily prolong your discussion, delaying progress either by over-thinking things or avoiding change.

As you prepare to read what follows, consider a few foundational leadership principles.

Keep the vision in mind. We have established why creating a strong community is important. As leaders, your next step is to develop a vision of your parish as a community of disciples. Make this personal. What would happen if more parishioners were involved; turned to each other in times of joy, grief, and need; readily invited others to come, serve, and lead; and accompanied one another on the journey of faith? Paint the picture in your mind's eye. Talk with others about this. Develop a compelling vision toward which you will aim as you take steps to make the vision reality.

Explore potential steps toward the vision. The steps included in this booklet are drawn from research as well as learning from parishes of all sizes, demographics, and expressions of parish life. As you read this book together, explore what already exists in your parish that contributes to life as a faith community. Identify possible ways that you can build on or learn from what is positively contributing. Consider asking parishioners for their input as you explore, offer a few focus groups, include a brief questionnaire in your bulletin or website, and speak with parishioners informally. Try not to be defensive when people offer ideas or criticism. Remember that they speak from their experience and perspective, and that their opinions may or may not be shared by others. If you regularly hear of an area that needs attention, keep this in mind as you discern your next steps. Even if there are good reasons for practices as they currently exist, it is important to acknowledge the perceptions of parishioners and, when possible, to address the needs they share.

Shape parish culture and practice. With the vision and potential steps firmly in mind, you can begin to shape the life of your parish for the future. Keep in mind that there are many small things you can do, even as you are reading and discussing this together. It will be helpful to not make too many changes all at once but rather to focus on one or two aspects of parish life, meet with the leaders in those areas, and work together to shape parish practice toward a more welcoming community of faith. Much of what follows points to the need to shape the culture of the parish as much as specific parish practices. Such culture change is a process that takes place over time. The conversations you have now, and the parish practices that emerge from those discussions, will contribute to the establishment of a culture of community in which people live as members of Christ's body together.

The sum is greater than the individual parts. Keep this always in your heart and mind. The things that you will do to build community have the potential to change someone's life, and the life of your parish. There is a cumulative nature to this: the sum of the changes you make and the new initiatives you begin will be much greater than the individual elements that are touched by your efforts. Just as the many parts of the body of Christ all contribute and are important in sharing and living the gospel, so too the many aspects of parish life that you have the opportunity to influence through your discussions, planning, and implementation.

Call forth and animate the gifts of all. This leads to the final foundational leadership principle, which is that your role as a leader is to call forth and animate the gifts of all in the parish. This is sometimes challenging for leaders who feel responsible for the many aspects of parish ministry that take place through parishioner involvement. What happens if someone doesn't follow through or has different ideas about how to proceed? We will explore this in much greater detail in the chapter of this book devoted to this topic. For now, be attentive to parishioners who may be ready to be involved or to deepen their involvement. Ask current ministry leaders to be on the lookout for others who may be ready to serve. Establish a shared expectation that all who are leaders will draw others to serve alongside them, so that there are no lone rangers in ministry. This will ensure that what happens at the parish is not limited by one person's reticence to share but rather expands as a result of the commitment of many.

While building community in the parish requires many people to work together, each of us has something special to contribute to the process. This book is your guide to eight things you can do, individually and with others, to shape the life of your parish and help it grow as a community of faith.

ONE

Embrace Servant Leadership

Do you recognize yourself as a leader? I often ask this question during parish leadership workshops and retreats and am struck by how many people who are parish staff members, or parishioners who are members of the parish council, committees, or coordinate ministries, do not consider themselves leaders. In their minds, the pastor is the one and only leader. All others carry out things the way the pastor directs. No doubt, the pastor is the leader of the parish. Yet anyone who in some way helps to shape or implement parish life is leading. Together, we influence the way in which our parish carries out Christ's mission of love and mercy. In this way, all of us are leaders who are responsible for actively participating in the parish by virtue of our baptism and who lead others to Christ through our words and witness.

Regardless of our role in the parish, leadership in the faith community is unlike leadership in any other organization. We are servants first, emulating the example and fulfilling the command given to us by Christ. Accepting a role of leadership in our parish amplifies and focuses our commitment to Christ as disciples. This servant leadership requires of us a different sort of sensibility in the ways in which we interact with others, particularly those with whom we minister and serve. Let us explore servant leadership and its implications in building the parish as a community of faith.

Servant leaders pray.

Our service and ministry, within our parish and beyond it, is an expression of our faith in God and commitment to follow Jesus. Understanding ourselves as servant leaders is a deepening of this commitment, often developing gradually over time. As servant leaders, we recognize with true humility that the ministry is not ours but Christ's. We invite Christ to work through us, and we rely on the Holy Spirit as we do so.

Our spiritual life, and certainly our ministry, is dependent upon and flows from a deep interior life in God. While any disciple might struggle with moments in which prayer takes a back seat, we who serve and lead in our parish must be especially mindful to remain rooted in prayer. One of the great challenges of parish ministry is that, while we help to foster spiritual growth for parishioners and provide opportunities for them to live and share their faith, doing so often results in a struggle to make time for prayer ourselves. A quote attributed to St. Francis de Sales illustrates this aptly: "Every one of us needs a half an hour of prayer each day, except when we are busy—then we need an hour." No matter how busy we find ourselves at home, in the workplace, in the local community, and in our parish, we cannot become too busy for God!

Through prayer, we discern the ways God is calling us to live, grow, and lead. In this prayerful discernment, we perceive the mission to which we are called and find the strength to live that mission in our daily lives, at our parish, and in the world. As Pope Francis says in *Rejoice and Be Glad*, "You too need to see the entirety of your life as a mission. Try to do so by listening to God in prayer and recognizing the signs that he gives you. Always ask the Spirit what Jesus expects from you at every moment of your life and in every decision you must make, so as to discern its place in the mission you have received. Allow the Spirit to forge in you the personal mystery that can reflect Jesus Christ in today's world" (GE, 23). Our mission is not divided into "personal" portions, or "parish" elements. We cannot be one sort of person at home and a very different sort at the parish. Rather, our personal spiritual lives, and our life at home, the parish, and in the world are all integrally connected—one mission in Christ Jesus.

All of the aspects of our lives are rooted in our relationship with God and nurtured in personal and communal prayer, particularly in the Sunday celebration of the Eucharist. The Eucharist most especially forms us as Christ's people. Through our participation in the Mass, we are drawn into communion with Christ and with one another. And we are shaped as a particular, local community, the body of Christ in this time and this place, together.

Servant leaders look to Jesus.

Parish ministry is an outgrowth of our relationship with Jesus. The longer we serve alongside others, the more we realize that we cannot invite people into a life we do not share with them. While we encourage all in our parish to follow Jesus with their lives, it is particularly crucial that we who lead look to Christ as our Savior and brother, and also as our teacher and model.

From the beginning of his public ministry, through his passion, death, and resurrection, Jesus teaches us what it is to be a servant leader. Jesus was always attentive to the other—people who would otherwise have been ignored, marginalized, or made scapegoats for the actions of those who were on the inside of the religious life of his time. Even when he was tired or wanted to pull away and have time with his disciples, Jesus ministered to those who needed him—the hungry, sick, grieving, and those who sought his teaching. Jesus drew people to himself—and to other people. He created a community of people who came to believe in him and sent them out as witnesses to his saving mercy. Jesus gave himself completely, and he found resurrection beyond the cross.

As servant leaders, we take to heart Jesus' example and grow in willingness to lay down our lives for the sake of others.

Servant leaders serve.

It might seem to go without saying that servant leaders serve. We offer our time, share our talents, and give of ourselves in ministry. Yet there is a quality to this service that shapes us over time. We grow as people who recognize Christ in the stranger, the outcast, the poor, and the alien, and who find joy in laying aside what we want in order to contribute to alleviating the needs of others. The service in which we share makes it possible for people to worship God, be shaped and fed by the Eucharist, learn about and grow in faith, and come together as Christ's people.

We do not do take the call to serve lightly, but rather, we embrace it out of a deep sense of responsibility. This is a sacred duty, borne of our baptism into Christ's body. In fact, we are co-responsible for the life of the parish. We fulfill this responsibility by collaborating with one another, drawing on one another's talents, and inviting others to serve with us. To collaborate is to co-labor, to work side-by-side. This form of leadership is about serving with, not standing apart from, others, as challenging, invigorating, and at times frustrating as that might be.

Servant leaders lead.

As in our own spiritual lives, leading a parish or a parish ministry is a process of discernment, through which we continually consider the ways we may witness to the astounding good news of Christ's love and share it with others through our parish groups, processes, and ministries. Reflect on your role in the parish and how you carry it out. In what ways do you serve? How do you lead? How might you be called to grow as a servant leader? What opportunities exist for you to draw others into leadership with you, to co-labor in order to shape your parish as a vibrant, living community of faith?

Servant leaders include others.

One of the greatest challenges of parish leadership is widening our view beyond the circle of people we know to include others in ministry and service. We naturally go to the people we know, with whom we are comfortable, and whom we know will get things done. Accepting responsibility as a servant leader involves widening our circles and taking a risk by inviting new people to serve with us. Be especially mindful to draw young people, teens and young adults, into leadership with you. They will bring fresh perspective, new ideas, and their peers, who will enliven your community with their enthusiasm.

Practical Ideas for Growing as a Servant Leader

Pray for your parish. Include your parish in your prayers, as you do family members and close friends.

Begin all meetings with prayer. Take time together to reflect on the Sunday readings. Allow this prayer and reflection to direct your ministry. Trust that the Holy Spirit will inspire and strengthen you as you build community within your parish.

Convene groups of leaders to discern direction together. It seems obvious, and yet often the obvious things must be stated clearly. We cannot discern direction for our parish just by ourselves! Bring groups of leaders together. Talk with one another about the vision of the parish as a community of believers and what it will take to build community within your parish.

TWO

Set the Tone

Clarify the vision of community for your parish. What do you mean when you say "community"? This is a necessary beginning point in the process of building community in the parish. While most of us have an image or an idea of what it means to be a strong community of faith, many find it difficult to articulate this in a clear and concise way. Perhaps it is challenging to express what we believe community to be about simply because growing as a community is such a complex, dynamic endeavor.

We know in our hearts that living as a community is more than simply getting along.

Being a Christian community is to be in communion with Christ and one another. This means that we hold out in front of ourselves the vision and goal of living as Christ taught us to live, and doing so together. Take time to talk with other leaders and clarify what it means to live as a community of faith in your time, place, and circumstances. Be specific. Create a compelling vision that you may share with others and strive toward in your attitudes, actions, and interactions with one another. Over time, become clear about what it will take to build community in your parish. What attitudes or behaviors are necessary in order to grow toward your vision?

Share the vision with others.
Are you part of a leadership group that is tasked with helping your parish grow as a community of faith? As you explore the various ways in which you may guide your parish toward the vision of becoming a strong Christian community, it will be crucial for you to share this vision with all in the parish, especially other leaders. Start with the pastoral council and staff, and include all who lead or are involved in parish groups and ministries. It is important that everyone in the parish understands this as a goal and expectation.

Invite those who serve in parish ministry to work on this. Help them to reflect on and recognize the impact of the parish in their lives and life of faith. Provide opportunities for them to think about the relationships that are central to their experience of the parish, and how these friendships are essential in the ways they endure hardship, experience joy, and everything in between. If the parish has such a positive impact on them, surely they will want this sort of deep relationship for others!

Identify the aspects of parish life that contribute to a strong sense of community now. Look at specific parish groups or ministries and people who model the sort of life-within-community to which you hope others will aspire. How might you build on these positive elements within your parish? What might you learn from these practices and the people who carry them out?

Be clear about the behaviors or attitudes that are contrary to the vision.

One of the most challenging aspects of leading the parish to grow as a community are the moments in which a person or group is clearly behaving in a way that is counter to this vision. As a friend recently noted, "Community is great, if it weren't for all the people!" She didn't really mean that, but her sentiment is well taken. Living in community with others requires us to be attentive to the needs of others, be mindful that our way is not the only way to do things, and remember that the purpose of the parish is to lead people to Christ and to living as disciples in the world. Plan ahead. What will you or another leader do when something happens that is not in keeping with the vision? Have strategies already in mind that will provide a means for a course correction for groups or a pastoral means for bringing individual people more fully into the process of building community.

Value everyone.

If we are to form our parish as a community, we must value every person—not only those who are similar to us, easy to like, and clearly on the path of discipleship. We must value everyone. This also means that we must have empathy for people in every age and stage of life and faith.

Look back at that fill-in-the-blank question at the beginning of this book. As you and those with whom you spoke filled in the blank, you were describing your parish's culture. Every parish has a culture, a certain way of being and living as Christian people together. Culture develops and is shaped by shared values and the behaviors necessary to carry out those values. When we speak of the parish having a culture, we recognize that our actions and attitudes have an impact on the way in which we carry out the mission of Christ within our parish and the course of our daily lives.

Culture often develops unintentionally. If a small group of people control most of what happens at the parish, the message is sent to others that their help is not needed. The resulting culture reinforces the notion that the parish is made up of insiders and outsiders. If you are committed to forming your parish as a community, this becomes a guiding value. Over time, all who lead and are involved must grow in commitment to building community. New processes are considered with this goal in mind, and current practices are aligned with it. The culture of the parish gradually shifts toward the development of a strong sense of community.

Be a tone-setter.

One of the most important things that you do as a leader is to set the tone in your parish and in parish ministries. This is where your leadership is essential in developing the sort of culture that will result in a strong community of faith. It is also where leading the parish requires the sort of servant leadership that we explored in the first chapter. A few examples:

- You are at a parish social event and are enjoying a great conversation with a group of friends. In the corner of your eye, you notice a parishioner who seems to want your attention. This particular parishioner seems to need a lot of attention, and you know that once you acknowledge her presence, it is likely that your visit with your friends will be over.

- You come into the parish office on Saturday morning, thinking that it is likely to be quiet and you can get a few things done. The phone rings, and the person answering the phone asks you to take the call.

- As a ministry coordinator, you are pleased that things are going really well. You have people in place to carry out all of the aspects of your ministry, and as a result, things seem to be humming along. You receive an email from the parish office, with the name of a new parishioner who has expressed interest in your ministry.

These are the sorts of situations that are part of every day in parish ministry. You know it well. While you read the examples above, you probably thought of a half dozen other situations to add to the list. Setting the tone requires the sort of response that is often nuanced, sometimes challenging, and often downright hard. You may want to turn your back on the needy parishioner while you spend time with friends, dodge taking that time-consuming phone call, and ignore the new parishioner who wants to get involved. As a tone-setter, however, you know what you must do: reach out to the needy one (even a brief greeting goes a long way); respond to the phone call with grace; invite the newcomer to join your ministry.

The truth is, when you set the tone well, others take note. They will follow your lead, and together you will shape the culture of your parish as a strong community of faith.

Practical Ideas for Setting the Tone

(PASTOR, STAFF, PARISHIONER MINISTER)

Think about the situations in which setting the tone is easy and those situations where it is more challenging. Find partners who with whom you can share, learn, and grow as tone-setters.

If you are reading this book with others, spend time talking with one another about what being a strong community would look like in your parish. Develop an "elevator pitch" in which you are able to articulate the vision of the parish as a community in three minutes or less.

Identify the attitudes, behaviors, and actions that will contribute to this vision of community. Name the groups, ministries, or people who contribute to the parish as a community now, and explore together the ways you may build on these positive contributors in the future.

Schedule time with parish leader groups, such as the parish council, to talk about building community within the parish. Develop a timeline with them for making this a priority and bringing the message to other leaders and to the wider parish.

Follow up on any comments you hear about the ways in which the parish culture contributes or fails to contribute to a strong sense of community.

THREE

Develop Communities within the Community

The parish is made up of people. I take note when I hear people say things like, "I wish the parish would..." or "The parish needs to..." or "I go to this parish..." as though "the parish" is separate and apart from the people that comprise it. When referring to "the parish," it is important to recognize that the people are the parish! There is a dramatic difference in the way people speak of the parish when they know it as their faith community. Suddenly, "the parish" becomes "our parish," or "my parish." No longer do they say, "I go to" this or that parish, but rather, "I belong to this parish." The person who is deeply rooted in the parish no longer thinks of it as a distant entity; rather, they understand that they have a part to play in making the parish what it can and should be—a family of faith. It is this shift from "the parish" to "our parish" that this book is all about.

Reflect on and learn from your experience.

How do you speak of your parish? When you think about your parish, what first comes to mind for you? The celebration of Mass is likely at the top of your list. Other things may come to mind as well, as you think of the ways your parish forms people in faith and leads them to serve others, especially as you recall moments in which they do so together.

I imagine that as you picture yourself at Mass, you also think of the people with whom you often gather. Some of the relationships you share with others at the parish may be the result of, or at least began in, a formal process such as a small faith community. Others may have developed informally as you became acquainted with each other at social events, while serving in the parish, or through the introduction of another parishioner.

Think for a moment about the ways you have met and grown in relationship with others at your parish. How did you meet? What led you to become acquainted and grow as friends? What were the things that connected you? The relationships you share with others at the parish make the faith community personal. When you have good friends at your parish, you know that they will be ready to accompany you on the journey of faith, sharing in your joys and trials with you, and you for them.

As we grow in relationship with others, the parish comes to feel like family, and as in our families, we do not choose all of the people with whom we interact. We meet and become friends with people who are very different from us. We encounter people with a wide range of experiences of life and faith. Even in passing conversations, we find ourselves sharing the impact of faith in the way we navigate the circumstances of our lives. And as we see the difference faith makes in the lives of other parishioners, we are inspired to grow and live in faith ourselves.

Make relationships a priority.

Often, we think of the friendships that form within the parish as a bonus—something nice that happens as we take part in parish events, ministries, and processes. If our goal is to form the parish as a community, however, we come to see such relationships as a priority rather than a nice by-product of parish life. As you consider the many ways people in your parish already become acquainted and form faith-filled friendships, think as well about how you might encourage other parish leaders to create opportunities within their groups for conversation, faith sharing, and relationship building.

Small is big.

In whatever way they are comprised, whether the choir, service project group, or small faith community, small groups build relationships among parishioners, so that rather than seeming large and impersonal, the parish feels smaller and more intimate. When we form friendships at the parish, it no longer seems a large, distant entity, but rather a part of our lives, the place where faith becomes real. When we consider the many ways parishioners become connected to each other, we easily see how many small groups and opportunities to build and develop relationships exist, and how these groups become "communities within the community" (see *The Joy of the Gospel*, 28). The stronger these groups and the relationships that come from them become, the stronger the parish community will be.

Small faith communities

Small groups come in all sorts of shapes and sizes and emerge in many different ways. Some are intentionally formed in order to bring people together with each other, explore and share faith, and apply faith to their daily lives. These small faith communities may draw people across generations together, or link people with similar needs or interests, such as mothers' and fathers' groups, daytime groups for retirees, support groups for people who are facing serious illness, grieving, or caring for aging parents. Small faith communities may begin with a series of seasonal gatherings or follow a once-per-month meeting format, yet the relationships that develop in them are often long lasting. As you explore the small groups in your parish and how people are invited and encouraged to join them, be attentive to opportunities to build on the experience of those who are part of groups already. Learn from them and encourage them to invite others to join their group or similar small communities in the future.

Ministry, service, and outreach groups

Many people meet and grow in friendship through participation in ministry, service, or outreach groups. Many warm and faith-filled friendships are born of participation in groups such as those who serve in liturgical ministries, those who take Holy Communion to the homebound, social action advocacy groups, parish committees, and so on. While many of these sorts of groups do not initially include an overt faith-sharing component, inviting members to think of and form themselves as communities within the community may enhance the benefits of participation for them, those who may join them, and all who are touched by their ministry.

Sacramental preparation

When we think of deep relationships that develop through participation in the parish, one of the first things that comes to mind for many is the RCIA. RCIA participants and team members often become close while growing in their appreciation for the faith over the course of the months or years of participation in the process. Think of the potential impact of a similar structure and design for other sacramental preparation processes (and remember that the RCIA is to be the inspiration for all catechesis). Perhaps you see signs of this sort of development already. How many lasting relationships among the participants and the wider community are begun in confirmation, marriage, and baptism preparation, among participants and their catechists, sponsors, and mentors? How might those who are responsible for sacramental preparation be encouraged to be mindful of the ways they might create opportunities for relationship building within the processes they guide?

Parents of children in religious education or the parish school

There are many opportunities for parents of children to meet each other—at the parish and in other aspects of their lives. Creating moments for faith sharing, conversation, and networking in already existing parent gatherings at the parish may result in faith-filled relationships that last far beyond an age or grade level. Not only do such relationships help the parents to feel part of the parish community long after their children have moved on to high school or college, they are crucial as the parents experience the challenges and joys of parenting during adolescence and emerging adulthood.

Faith mentors and spiritual companions

Does your parish invite people to accompany one another in faith as mentors or spiritual companions? While few parishes have any formal process for helping people to form such intentional, faith-driven relationships, there is much evidence that suggests the potential benefit, especially for but not limited to relationships between adults and young people.

Practical Ways to Form Communities within the Community

Be intentional about the ways you invite people to grow in Christian love for each other.

Use examples in homilies, meetings, and parish communication. Invite people to share brief witness talks, before or at the end of Mass, in which they share the impact of the parish on their lives and faith.

Whenever possible, cross invisible boundary lines. Create opportunities for people to meet and share faith with others across generations, ethnic groups, and life experience.

Do a "relationship audit" that helps you identify all of the many ways people become acquainted and develop friendships at your parish. How might you help people to become more attentive to the importance of their faith-filled relationships and the ways they might connect people with one another at the parish?

FOUR

Open Doors

Is your parish warm and welcoming? A few years ago, I was invited to present a Saturday workshop for leaders at a parish, focusing on building a strong parish community. Those who gathered seemed very interested in making their parish an inviting community of faith. Like many groups of parish leaders, they expressed concern that the same group of people seemed to bear the weight of the parish through ministry and financial giving, and they shared their frustrations in trying to engage others in the life of the church. Throughout the day, they also spoke of how they felt their parish already was hospitable, warm, and welcoming.

The workshop ended late Saturday afternoon, and I remained at the parish to attend the Saturday evening Mass. Imagine my surprise, and dismay, when no one smiled, said hello, offered me a worship aid, or extended a welcome as I entered the church. I sat for a few moments, prepared myself for Mass, and then walked to the back doors of the church, found the worship aids, and distributed them to others who, like me, had arrived through the side doors. It seems those who came to the workshop did not clearly see their parish from the perspective of a guest, or a side-door participant. Their perception was based solely on their limited, personal, "back door" experience.

Open the doors literally, and more!

When we think of hospitality and welcome, our initial thoughts immediately focus on greeting those who come to Sunday Mass. Surely, this is crucial—the way in which we greet people at Mass is a sign of our desire that all who come to us will find genuine warmth and care, a community that hopes that they will come to belong with us in Christ. The way we welcome people as they gather for Mass is a firm foundation upon which we may build community in our parish. Not only this. Our Sunday hospitality sets the standard and provides an internal image for the ways in which we welcome, offer care, and reach out with compassion, greeting people as Christ among us every day of the week.

At Sunday Mass, ensure that ministers of hospitality are at all doors of the church. Whenever possible, the doors should be open, inviting people to come in. Even better, a few hospitality ministers can be stationed outside the doors of the church, helping those who need assistance as they leave their cars, and extending a warm greeting to all as they enter. Even in large parishes, hospitality ministers become familiar with those who regularly attend a particular liturgy. They recognize visitors or new parishioners and may extend a special greeting to them, ensuring that they know where hymnals or worship aids are located, and briefly sharing any special details that will help them enter more fully into the celebration. They may introduce themselves and the other ministers who are nearby, or invite them to connect after Mass, when they may introduce the newcomer to the priest, deacon, and/or parishioner leaders who are present.

Everyone contributes and is responsible for opening doors.

At the parish where I served as a staff member, we began a process for inviting people to inquire about our Catholic faith that we called "Open Door." The concept was very simple. Announcements were made at the end of Mass and in the bulletin that sounded a bit like this: "There's always an open door here. If you or someone you know is interested in exploring Catholicism, has been away from the Church for some time and is considering returning, or perhaps has questions, we invite you to gather with a group of caring people." The details of a gathering were provided, and parishioners were invited to share the invitation with their family members, friends, and neighbors. The sessions were held three times a year, just after Christmas, during the Easter season, and in the early autumn.

Not only were the gatherings grace-filled opportunities to greet people and offer a genuine welcome, we heard from many parishioners that they suddenly realized that they have a responsibility to open doors for the people in their lives. They invited friends to come to the Open Door gathering, but that was just the beginning. Parishioners took to heart the call to build the kind of community of which people would want to be a part. Some talked with hospitality ministers or called the office to ask how they could become more involved. Offering an "open door" turned out to be a powerful image for building community for our parish.

Perception is everything.

While it is not possible for us to completely grasp the experience of guests or newcomers to our parish, we can, and must, do what we can to look at the parish through the eyes of those who are visitors or those who are not already involved. This is one way in which parish culture really matters. If those who come to Mass for the first time experience a closed door (literally or figuratively), they are likely to never return. If those who are ready to join the parish cannot figure out when or where registration is available, they may find a different parish, come to Mass but not become rooted as members, or simply drift away. A parish staff person once told me that her parish is warm and welcoming but that others perceive it as closed and uncaring. I could not help but reply that in the case of hospitality, perception is everything.

Open doors for newcomers.

One of the most fruitful ways for building community is to engage newcomers to the parish while they are still new. They have made a conscious decision to join us; they may be new to our city or area, or they may be in a life transition, entering a new career or job, or preparing for marriage or the baptism of a child. They might have recently retired and relocated to be near their family. Whatever brings them to our parish, we have a great opportunity to open doors for them, inviting them to meet other parishioners, join a parish ministry, and offer their ideas for strengthening the parish. New members have not yet grown accustomed to the "way we have always done things," and therefore provide valuable perspective.

Practical Ideas for Opening Doors

Do a walk-through of the parish grounds through the eyes of visitors. Is it easy to find restrooms, the parish office, common meeting rooms, etc.? Be attentive to signage and the natural ways people move from one space to another. Are there common entrances that are not clearly marked? What about physical access for those with special mobility needs?

Form a group to review your processes for registering and welcoming new members. Ensure that opportunities to join the parish are regularly made available and that hospitality ministers and other parish leaders know how to direct newcomers. Be sure to include follow-up in your plan. If a new member offers his or her time in a parish ministry or shares a pastoral need, make sure someone follows up in a timely manner.

Create a welcoming process with a personal touch. Form a team who will host neighborhood gatherings, call new parishioners, and/or invite new members to join parish ministries. Ask new parishioners to join the team and share their ideas for enhancing the way people are welcomed throughout their first six months at the parish.

FIVE

Be Attentive

Have you ever walked into a room full of strangers and felt invisible? Put yourself in this situation: no one seemed to notice you, there was no cordial greeting, no friendly introduction, no invitation to join a conversation, sit at table, or take part in an activity. The hosts are busy placing food on tables and often disappear into the kitchen. Everyone else seems to know one another, and they are totally absorbed in their conversations. Now, imagine someone walking up to you with welcome in his or her eyes. Feel the relief as you are included, the acceptance that makes the room suddenly seem warm with kindness and friendship.

As parish leaders, we have the opportunity to make this sort of difference for people in our parish, whether parishioners or visitors, those who participate in ministry or those who are recipients of service. When we pause and reflect on it, this is clear. Yet most of us can admit that we are not always as attentive as we can be. We may be pressed for time or focused on something that truly needs completion. In fact, we may find ourselves grumbling, whether aloud or to ourselves, when someone interrupts our "progress." When we are at our busiest and most stressed, we must remember that the interruptions are, indeed, our ministry. In the words of C.S. Lewis, "The great thing, if one can, is to stop regarding all the unpleasant things as interruptions of one's 'own,' or 'real' life. The truth is of course that what one calls the interruptions are precisely one's real life—the life God is sending one day by day: what one calls one's 'real life' is a phantom of one's own imagination" (*Yours, Jack: Spiritual Direction from C.S. Lewis*). To embrace this sort of approach to life and ministry, we must be attentive. By paying attention, we will ensure that our parish will be a community in which no one is invisible and everyone is valued as a child of God.

Be attentive to people.

One of the most compelling things we learn from the gospels is how attentive Jesus was to people. Jesus often stopped what he was doing to attend to the needs of people, especially the sick, grieving, and vulnerable, among the crowds or alone and lonely. Jesus stopped what he was doing to reach out with care, compassion, and mercy. As followers of Jesus, we look to his example and know that people must come first, especially those who might otherwise go unnoticed.

Attending to those who come and go

It is easy for many in our parishes to come and go. Often, they give the impression that they like it this way—they arrive at Mass just before the gathering song, and they leave as soon as the final blessing has been offered. We are challenged to connect with these not-engaged people. A smile, greeting, or handshake go a long way. We never know when that small sign of care will bear fruit. Often, in a moment of need, no matter how involved a person may have previously been or have not been, he or she realizes that the community is committed to sharing Christ's love, and that inspires fuller participation in the future. Perhaps a person came to the parish when a family member became ill or died. Perhaps the care your community showed them at that time helped them realize the blessing of being more deeply rooted in the community. In time, the person may become ready to join a parish group.

Attending to those who linger

Do you sometimes notice people who seem to be waiting for an invitation to participate? You may think to yourself that there are many opportunities to get involved. All one needs to do is listen to the announcements or read the bulletin. Yet we all know that a personal invitation is much more effective. Even if we do not know the person, being attentive to those who linger after Mass, come to parish socials (perhaps without speaking to others), or participate in service opportunities can be for them and the parish a sharing of God's grace.

Attending to those who are demanding

Wait, you might be thinking. How can I not pay attention to those who are demanding? They are always present, and always in need of someone's time. These might be the very vulnerable among us, or those who are emotionally fragile. They might be the fussy ones who seem to always have a bone to pick, or they may be people who constantly need affirmation. The demanding ones need a particular sort of attention—caring, compassionate, and pastorally sensitive. Again, we look to Jesus. He sought out those who needed him, and he responded to the ones who came to him in need. Yet when we read the gospels carefully, we also realize Jesus tended to their needs and then sent them out to share the Good News with others. He did not allow those who were able to remain stuck in their previous situation. Those who are part of parish ministries that tend to parishioners in need can learn from Jesus' example by developing strategies for pastoral response that respects the person, establishes boundaries, and encourages self-sufficiency. Pastoral ministers must also develop skills and know local resources for referral as appropriate.

Be attentive to the spiritual needs of parishioners.

As we reflect on the ways we may build community in the parish, it is important to be mindful that the parish is the place that most Catholics rely on for their spiritual nourishment and development. This is especially so at Sunday Mass. We do well to form the parish as a community in which people are helped to make connections between their experience of the Sunday liturgy and the rest of their lives. Parishioners will benefit from opportunities for faith formation—not only processes that lead them to grow in knowledge of the faith, but also opportunities to explore ways to pray, learn from the saints and spiritual masters, and integrate spirituality into their daily lives. By paying attention to people's spiritual needs at the various ages and stages of life and faith, we will more readily grow as a community of faith.

Be attentive to the needs of those beyond the parish.

There is no doubt that Christians are called to care for the poor, ill, imprisoned, grieving, immigrants, and vulnerable. The more attentive we are to the needs of those beyond the parish, and the more we invite parishioners to grow in their commitment to share Christ's love, forgiveness, mercy, and compassion, the greater the sense of community will be in the parish. Such service becomes an expression of the growing faith of individuals and the parish. Parishioners come to see themselves as part of a community that lives as Christ teaches. They grow in relationship with one another and experience God's love as they share that love with others.

Be attentive to those we can connect through introduction or invitation to serve together.

Are you a connector? Do you know someone who is? While we may strategize about ways to build community within our parish, and rightly so, it is essential for us to recognize as well the "special something" that happens when relationships develop and friendships grow within the parish. As leaders, we must be attentive to those whom we might connect with each other. Not everyone does this naturally. If this is not your strength, find people who revel in bringing others together, and encourage them to share their talent by paying attention to those they might introduce to others. The lives of individuals and the parish will be strengthened through such person-to-person connections.

Practical Ideas for Being Attentive

Ensure that everyone in the parish knows who to call with pastoral needs. Some parishes have a hotline that people may call when in need of material or physical support, such as food, clothing, and housing. Many parishes have a group that coordinates rides to the doctor, hospital, or grocery for homebound parishioners, or those who are experiencing a short-term medical condition.

If the parish has spiritual directors or pastoral counselors, make sure parishioners know how to contact these people; if the parish does not have such support, create lists of people to whom parishioners may be referred.

Ask parishioners for their ideas and input about the impact of existing ministries that serve the needs of parishioners and people beyond the parish.

Create a form that regularly appears in the bulletin or a suggestion box that is placed in the gathering space of the church to invite parishioners to share their insights about what is working and what is needed for the future.

Start running a column in the parish bulletin in which parishioners may briefly share their experience in serving or being served through parish ministries.

SIX

Call Forth and Animate the Gifts of All

One of the greatest obstacles to building community in the parish is the perception that often develops that everything is fine just the way it is. "We've always done it this way." "We have everything under control and do not need any help." As I have spoken with parish leaders about this, I have heard two common responses.

On one side, those who are already involved feel a strong sense of responsibility for what happens at the parish. Often, they were personally invited to serve or lead by the pastor or a good friend, and they feel that what they are doing is fulfilling that request. Without intending to have a negative impact, these very responsible people sometimes also limit the ways others can be involved. They are concerned that there will not be enough follow-through, or that the newcomers will do things differently from the way they have been done in the past. Sometimes, they understand the need to involve new people, but feel that doing so unnecessarily complicates things. You may be nodding your head at this moment, recalling a time when it happened just this way.

The flip side of this situation is that those who offer their help may have been told they are not needed. This might not have been communicated verbally, but it often happens when people are invited to sign up for a parish ministry or group and then receive no call to serve: "I offered my help once, or more often, but never received a call, so I gave up."

Both of these reactions are understandable. And both must be addressed if our parish is to grow as a community. The way we call forth and animate the gifts of all is at the heart of building community in the parish.

Establish a culture in which everyone is invited to serve.

Of all of the things we can do to shape the culture of our parish and build community, inviting everyone to serve must be near the top of the list. In fact, there is much statistical evidence that points to the importance of this, as well our own personal stories, which help us to understand the impact of meaningful involvement in the parish. As we build community, we are establishing a culture in which people understand that our parish hopes and expects that every person will give of him or herself in service, caring, and sharing, and that doing so is an expression of our commitment to Christ. We establish a culture in which everyone knows "this is what it means to be a Christian as a member of this parish community."

As we have already noted, inviting everyone to serve is often easier said than done. There are two primary challenges, each of which has a companion "solution."

The first challenge is convincing parishioners to give of their time and talent in ministry and service. The "solution" is to help people embrace stewardship as a way of life. This is a long-term strategy rather than a temporary fix. Often, parishes focus on how we need parishioners to give: "the parish needs you to get involved," or "the parish needs your financial giving." When forming our people as stewards, we help them to recognize that they have a need to give. The difference is remarkable. No matter how we couch the "give to a need" plea, it is a functional request that has little connection to our relationship with Christ and is therefore a short-term strategy at best. Helping people to grow in gratitude for their many blessings and to recognize their "need to give," on the other hand, has deep and lasting spiritual implications in the lives of parishioners, and long-term impact on the parish.

The second challenge is related to the first, and that is helping all who are already involved in ministry to warmly welcome newcomers and to provide opportunities for them to give of themselves in meaningful ways. The "solution" to this challenge is to help leaders recognize the impact of serving in the parish in their own lives, and to establish an expectation that they will provide opportunities for people to serve meaningfully along-side them.

As leaders, we have a blessed responsibility to create a culture in which everyone is invited to give of his or her talents in ministry. I am not naive about the challenges of adopting the "solutions" above. But I have also seen and experienced the impact of doing so—in my own life and in the lives of countless parish communities. Reflect on this in your own experience. Who first invited you to serve in parish ministry? What has been the impact for you in being involved, serving side by side with other parishioners?

Look for those who seem ready to become involved or to deepen their involvement.

Remember the idea of being attentive to those who linger? It is very likely that those who remain after Mass, perhaps offering their help in tidying up after a large event, or who come to parish socials (even without talking with anyone while there) may be looking for a way to make a connection with others at the parish. They may serve eagerly if and when they are invited to do so. I find that many of the most involved and engaged parishioners began in just this way. Often, they tell me that they were unsure if an announcement applied to them—they did not really understand what is involved in getting involved! Be attentive as well to those who give of their time in one-time or seasonal projects. They may be ready to deepen their commitment through ongoing involvement in ministry.

Be a talent scout.

Have you ever invited someone to get involved, only to be met with a polite decline to the invitation? Most of us have had this experience, and for many leaders the experience of being turned down sticks in our memory and makes us less willing to invite others in the future. People are far more likely to accept an invitation when they feel their particular talents or skills are needed or that their service would be in an area of interest or passion. Consider this from your own perspective. How much more likely would you be to respond to an invitation that begins something like this: "I have noticed that you are often at the 8:00 Mass and you greet those around you with a wonderful smile. Have you ever considered being a minister of hospitality? Your smile would go a long way in helping others feel welcome here." Or, "I remember when we served on a school committee together a few years ago. You were always the most organized among us. Would you consider offering your organizational talent for our parish festival committee? You wouldn't be alone—we have many others who are involved, and we would really be grateful if you would join us!"

Part of our role as parish leaders is to call forth the gifts of people within the community and to help them to give of themselves in meaningful ways. This means that we must become adept at recognizing talent in others and inviting them to give those talents in ministry and service. People often have difficulty in naming their own talents. Many have grown up being taught to not draw attention to what they do well. Rather than helping people to grow in humility, this is really about false humility—the truly humble person recognizes that all we are and have comes from God, and in giving back we give glory to God who is the giver of all good things. When we help people know that the things they naturally do well are talents, and when we provide opportunities for them to give their talents in meaningful ways, our "talent scouting" has lasting impact—on individuals and the parish community.

Help other leaders to become talent scouts as well. If you are looking for people for a specific ministry or task, identify the talents that are needed. Ask people to be on the lookout for parishioners who have the sort of talent you seek: someone who naturally relates well with others, a person who is known as someone who always gets things done, someone who easily communicates and drives a message home, a person who loves to plan or to carry out a plan, for example. Then, invite the people with the talent and help them see how their ministry would make a difference.

Encourage and thank those who serve.

Often, those who are most involved are the ones who least often receive expressions of gratitude. Unfortunately, we sometimes take each other for granted. It is important to understand that thanking people is a way to help them know that their contributions make a difference. If we hope to help people grow in gratitude for all they are and have, and to offer themselves and their resources as an expression of thankfulness, we must begin by encouraging and thanking those who serve in our parish community. No matter how it is expressed, "thank you" goes a long way in building a community of people who recognize that the parish is what it is because of the selfless giving of those who offer themselves in service, within the parish and beyond it.

Create a process through which people may discern involvement in ministry with others.

Value prayerful discernment that includes stepping back from ministry when members feel called to do so. Remember those people noted above, who feel responsible for parish groups or ministries and therefore turn others away? Some of them (maybe you in one or more ministry) stay in their role out of a sense of responsibility, not because they feel they have the talents that would be most beneficial, or even because they have a real passion for the ministry. When we begin to help each other discern a good fit in ministry and establish the understanding that it is good to step back when we feel called to do so, we strengthen the ministry and the parish.

Practical Ways to Call Forth and Animate the Gifts of All

Talk with other leaders about the expectations you have for parishioner involvement. The parish will grow as a community in direct proportion to the ways in which parishioners grow in understanding of themselves as stewards, and of the parish as a community of disciples who give of themselves and their resources as a response to the love of God.

Establish terms for leadership roles. Doing so ensures that many people will have the opportunity to contribute their ideas, time, and talents.

If your parish does not currently have a process for forming people as stewards, consider creating a stewardship committee to facilitate this process.

Explore processes to help parishioners identify and use their talents. This is a key way to help parishioners bring faith to their daily lives, and it renews the parish in the process.

Some parishes have a small "ministry coordinator" ministry, through which people may discern a good fit, find others who may be called to serve, and create processes for ministry mentoring, shadowing, formation, and training.

SEVEN

Develop a Strong Sense of Mission

When the parish understands itself as the People of God, members of Christ's body who are called to share God's love in the world, this mission drives everything that happens at the parish. Living as people of mission together fills the community with a sense of purpose—when we are clear about our mission, we understand the reason for all of the tasks, activities, and projects at the parish. The mission becomes our reference point.

Having this clear sense of mission is essential in engaging people in the life of the parish and, through the parish, the Christian life. There are many things that young people are teaching us and that they ask us to take seriously. Among these is a desire to give toward something that matters. Another way of saying this is that today's young people (to be honest, most of us) have many things vying for their time. They do not want to commit their time and attention to things that won't make a difference in the lives of people or in the life of the world.

Don't misunderstand; surely young people and all of us spend time doing inconsequential things, and sometimes doing so is crucial to our well-being. There is much wisdom in keeping Sabbath—taking time away with God and away from the stress of work. Yet, most of us can appreciate the desire to know that one's efforts will matter. We want to be part of something that is bigger than ourselves, to live our Christian faith in truly integrated and authentic ways, and to be with others who are also living with this sense of purpose and meaning.

Live Christ's mission, together.

When we invite and encourage people to become more deeply rooted in the community, and to serve within the parish, we are asking them to understand that doing so is a way of contributing to Christ's mission and to their mission as Christ's people. The more we live in mission at the parish, the more likely parishioners will see themselves as disciples in mission in all of the aspects of their lives. We might say that this is where faith becomes real, because this sense of mission affects the dozens of decisions we make each day, about who we are as God's people, what we are called to be about, how we will interact with others, and what we will spend our time doing. Living as people of mission is a profoundly meaningful way of life, contagious in its depth and joy.

The dreaded mission statement

Understanding the importance of having clarity in mission is what prompts many parishes to adopt a mission statement. The statement is often developed through a series of meetings among parish leaders, and at best, it provides a clear and succinct articulation of how the parish understands itself as a community of disciples. The process of developing the mission statement is only the beginning. Once the parish is clear about the mission, all plans, ministries, groups, and activities must be aligned with the mission. This brings us back to the importance of having a clear vision for the parish—the vision is the mission, and the mission is the vision.

It doesn't always happen this way, however. At times, the development of the mission statement becomes an exercise in futility. After arduous meetings and multiple discussions, a statement, often long and rambling, is written, perhaps placed on the cover of the bulletin, and nothing happens as a result. Sometimes, the mission statement does drive some parish activity in the first year following development, and then it fades in consciousness as the parish and its people go on about their daily lives. Parishioner leaders sometimes wince when I mention mission for these very reasons. Why put so much time and energy into developing something that does not have lasting impact?

Some parish leaders question why a mission statement is needed. Isn't the mission the gospel? In one sense this is true—it is one mission, which is Christ's mission in the world. Yet, it is important to be clear about how this will be done, in your particular time, place, and circumstances.

Be intentional; stay focused.

Living and growing as disciples of Jesus Christ is a lifelong endeavor. As Christian people, we are called to become more like Christ throughout the days, weeks, months, and years of our lives. Our parish community has much to offer us in this life of conversion in Christ. As leaders, we help to shape our parish, so that the very life of the community is formative. Such leadership requires us to be intentional in the way we lead people to understand that they are created in God's image, called to holiness, drawn to Christ through baptism, called to live as disciples, and are temples of the Holy Spirit whose lives may give praise and glory to God.

Most parishes have many elements of life that serve to form people as disciples. The Eucharist and sacraments are key, and all that we do to help people to reflect upon and grow in their participation in the liturgy is sure to bear great fruit. Faith formation, for children, young people (teens and young adults) and adults, holds great potential for helping people to grow throughout the ages and stages of their lives and faith. The many ways we invite people to give of themselves in ministry, service, and outreach form people as disciples and urge them to express their commitment to Christ in action.

Words matter.

If you had asked my mother why she selflessly gave her time to an elderly parishioner who did not drive, or why serving at the local soup kitchen was such an important part of her life, she would have said that these sorts of things are simply what you do as a Catholic. I know because I heard people ask her this over the years, and I was always struck by her simple response. I don't think I ever heard her use the words "discipleship," "stewardship," or "ministry," and yet her life spoke of all of these realities. But my mother lived in a different age. Some call our era "post-Christian." We may no longer assume that those who are baptized, receive First Holy Communion, and are confirmed will continue to actively practice their faith in their adult years. Our surrounding culture is often ambivalent about faith, and certainly so about organized religion. In our time, and perhaps in my mother's as well, there is great benefit to connecting what we teach and celebrate and how we live, and to being able to articulate why doing so has an impact on our daily lives.

Words matter in this regard. The more deeply we understand ourselves as disciples, the more readily we turn our hearts and lives to Christ; the more fully we grasp that we are blessed with life, talents, faith, and resources, the more likely we will be to share those blessings with others as good stewards; the more we grasp Christ's command to serve the least among us, the more we will grow in willingness to lay down our lives for the sake of others. When we use words such as "disciple," "steward," and "ministry" well and purposefully, we grow as a parish community in mission.

Practical Ways to Develop a Strong Sense of Mission

Assess your parish's sense of mission with others. If your parish has a mission statement, is it clear, concise, and memorable? Is it the reference point for all parish ministry and activity? If your parish does not have a mission statement or if your current statement is out of date or does not direct parish life and ministry, plan to discuss this with your pastor and pastoral council in the future.

Lead already-involved parishioners to deepen their understanding of mission, ministry, and service. Hold annual retreats for leaders to form them as disciples, to enhance their understanding of themselves as leaders, and to help them grow in skill as they fulfill their roles within the parish.

Establish patterns of peer-to-peer mentoring in parish groups and ministries. Tie the ways people serve to the parish mission.

Create an environment in which parishioners are encouraged to discern the ways God is calling them to live, love, lead, and participate in the mission of Christ through the parish community.

EIGHT

Become a Community that Journeys in Faith Together

Return once again to that fill-in-the-blank question at the beginning of this book. Does your response change as a result of your reading and conversations with others? Do you have a different vision for the way you hope others will respond in the future? What do you mean when you speak of building community in your parish?

Of all of the images of the life of Christian discipleship that we might use to guide our conversations and planning, I still find the image of journey most helpful. It is a metaphor we have often used to describe the life of conversion to which we are called. Some might find it a bit tired or worn, and yet it is descriptive of the process of living and growing as a follower of Jesus Christ. The truth is, living and growing as a disciple is the work of a lifetime. It is not exactly the same for any two people, and yet there are common challenges and joys, questions, doubts, and assurances in faith. When we journey in faith together in community, we hold each other up in times of distress, share in one another's joys, encourage each other to grow in relationship with God, and challenge one another to live as committed disciples.

The steps we have explored in this book are precisely that—steps on the journey within the parish that will help us to grow as a community of faith. There is a cumulative nature to what we have explored here—one step taken will affect more than the aspect of parish life involved. When we positively touch people in the way they live faith in their daily lives, the impact is immeasurable, within the parish and beyond it.

Share faith.

With whom do you share your journey of faith? Who knows your story? Whose sharing inspires, encourages, or strengthens you? It is one thing to speak of the parish as a faith community. It is quite another thing when the parish actually begins to grow in this way! As you strive to build community in your parish, be mindful of all of the ways you may encourage people to become comfortable sharing their faith with others.

Play together.

My pastor is fond of telling people that we have to play together as well as pray together. This seems a fitting way to remind ourselves that part of being community is being together! Parishes often have a few social gatherings that are part of the life of the parish. Festivals, dinners, coffee and doughnuts, fish frys. Don't underestimate the impact of these social moments. Some parishes are very intentional in the way social gatherings help to build community, by including name tags, inviting people to contribute a favorite dish, or contribute something from their ethnic group. These times of being together just for the sake of being together are often the times when new parishioners first come to meet others. When you speak of "community" with the average parishioner, it is likely that many will speak of such gatherings. They may share how they met someone at a dinner years ago, then recognized them at Sunday Mass, and then found themselves serving side by side in a parish ministry.

Practical Ways to Become a Community that Journeys in Faith Together

Offer annual retreats, through which people may encounter Christ and grow in faith. Many peer-led retreats include faith witness talks, which inspire participants and help team members become more comfortable sharing their faith journey with others.

Include faith sharing at parish meetings through reflection on the Sunday readings. Such spiritual formation drives the activity of the group over time and creates a bond among those involved.

Occasionally invite parishioners to share faith witness talks before or at the end of Sunday Mass. These talks might be focused on stewardship, the impact of the RCIA, or faith in general. Such witnesses inspire others to share their faith journey, and the parish grows in its understanding of itself as a community of faith.

Look at your parish calendar for the coming year. Are there opportunities for people to gather socially at least once a quarter? Are a variety of people involved in organizing and carrying out these social gatherings? Is there a group or segment of the parish that is not included, overtly or through oversight?